There are two points of advantage from which to get impressive views of the nave; first by standing under the central tower and looking west – as seen on the front flap of this book – culminating at the west window; the other by standing on the west steps and looking east towards the stalls and the choir screen as in the picture on the left. **The Cathedral** is in the centre of the city and is felt to be a homely place. It is entered from the thoroughfare and this is suggestive. Some cathedrals have lawns and paths to traverse before entering; we are immediately in contact with the moving life. There is reason for withdrawal and an equal advantage in close contacts; a step from the street brings you into the building.

We enter the cathedral thinking of its history. In one form or another it has stood here for 900 years. From 1092 until 1540 it was the Abbey of St Werburgh, a Benedictine monastery founded by Hugh Lupus, Norman Earl of Chester, assisted by St Anselm. In the reign of Henry VIII the monasteries were dissolved. This became the Cathedral Church for the newly formed diocese of Chester, and its dedication changed to that of Christ and the Blessed Virgin Mary, and thus it has remained with the Bishop's throne, and served by a Dean, Canons and other clergy. This indicates a continuous witness to Christian faith and life. Prior to the Norman Abbey there was a Saxon church founded by Ethelfleda for secular canons and possibly a smaller church before that. From the past we turn to the present. Parts of the building are obviously Norman, but in the thirteenth century the rebuilding and extension of the Abbey was begun when Simon de Whitchurch was abbot and this went on intermittently until just before the Dissolution. The Nave was begun in 1349 when Richard de Seynesbury was abbot, and finished some two hundred years later. In the last century there was a great restoration and now extensive repairs are in hand; work goes on, for the maintenance of the fabric is a great responsibility.

ABOVE The **West Window** – constructed in 1961; beautiful glass replaced the window damaged in the war. The main lights depict the Blessed Virgin; Holy Child; St Joseph; surrounding are Northern Saints; symbols of the apostles and Divine inspiration.

LEFT We approach to view the great glory of the Cathedral, the Choir and the Stalls. But first we see the **Choir Screen** and the Organ near by. It is good at this point to look around; we are beneath the central tower. The figures of the Rood were carved in 1913 in what is now the Italian Tyrol and their significance is immense. Looking westward you are near the new Stalls at the end of the Nave and by the Altar. These stalls for the Bishop and the Chapter are an excellent example of adaptation of seventeenth-century woodwork remade by our craftsmen, and cleaned. Beyond are new stalls for the choir. All these commemorate a former Dean, Michael Gibbs (d. 1962).

LOWER LEFT **The ceiling of the Central Tower:** The ceiling is supported by two fifteenth-century transverse arches. They constitute a rare architectural feature and have been described as a 'crown-work of stone'. The ceiling, of pitch-pine, dates from 1819 and was made by two Chester joiners to the specification of Thomas Harrison, the famous Chester architect. In 1969 the ceiling was repaired and decorated in a red and gold pattern under the direction of George Pace. Modern lighting techniques were at the same time installed and it is now possible to see the ceiling properly from the floor of the crossing. Prior to 1969 it was virtually in permanent darkness.

UPPER RIGHT We pass through the gates to **The Choir,** built in the thirteenth century, replacing that of the Norman foundation. Later that century the enlargement of the Abbey was started by Simon de Whitchurch, and the reconstruction of the entire east end. In this Choir we see stonework seven hundred years old, and 'it is a beautiful example of the transition from the Early English to the Decorated style of architecture'. The magnificent canopied **Stalls** in carved woodwork deserve close attention; they are still much as they were 600 years ago when provided for the monastery. The late F. H. Crossley wrote: 'Craftsmen and carpenters capable of designing and making such work were in good supply, and their ingenuity was apparently inexhaustible. The tall spires rising from a forest of pinnacles decorating the niches and canopies were the secret of medieval art unsurpassed since, and not thought of before.'

LOWER RIGHT **The Misericords** are most interesting, being as old as the stalls with a variety of carving, here as elsewhere. Each one has a dual seat for relaxation in worship. This illustration shows one which tells the legend of St Werburgh and the Geese.

Chester: Cathedral and City

Described by C. E. Jarman

Canon Emeritus of Chester and

photographed by R. H. Tilbrook

A JARROLD COLOUR PUBLICATION

The pictures on the cover will have interested you and aroused curiosity; they illustrate Chester. We enjoy seeing historic places on the spot or on television, but there is a place for pictorial reproduction in book form. Chester is renowned and visitors can see in walking round the survival of much that is ancient, whilst redevelopment adds the competence of our time without destroying the qualities of the past. There is continuity. The Britons named this place Caerlyon for as Higden the medieval chronicler – of whom more later – wrote, 'This cyte in tyme of Britons was hede and chyefe cyte of all Venedocia (North Wales). Thys cyte in Brytyshe spech bete Carthleon. Chestre in Englyshe and Cyte of Legyons also. For there laye a wynter of legyons . . . sent for to wyne Irlonde.'

Nearly 2000 years have passed since the Roman legion made a fortress on 'a low sandstone hill at the head of the estuary of the Dee and called the station Deva'. Its key position to the Roman soldiers meant that it became a military and commercial centre, the headquarters of the XX Roman Legion in Britain. The legion was withdrawn about A.D. 400 and the protection it had given to these parts ceased, the fortress deserted and the Britons exposed to the incursions of Saxons and Scots. We have Roman remains in several places. Ethelfrith, pagan King of Northumbria in A.D. 615, fought with the Welsh and the city was destroyed and lay in ruins. It was derelict when in 894 a Danish army wintered here, and this prompted Ethelred and Ethelfleda to rebuild the walls and found places of Christian worship. The years passed. In late Saxon times Chester gained in reputation, having its own mint and a sturdy independence was emerging. The Palatine Earldom was created after the Norman Conquest. At first the Conquest was resisted and then accepted. Cheshire became a county palatine and Chester the seat of government of the palatine earls. Prince Charles is Earl of Chester as well as Prince of Wales. It is an ancient title and he has a long line of predecessors.

Chester had its great days of medieval prosperity in the thirteenth and early fourteenth centuries; there was a flourishing port and trade was good. But its fortunes changed and it began 'to lose its standing as a port through the gradual silting up of the Dee estuary and the city was further impoverished by the inroads of the Welsh'. Many charters were granted by English monarchs to the citizens, and there were charters to the Benedictine Abbey of St Werburgh, now the Cathedral. In the thirteenth century it is said 'the religious life of Chester and indeed its economic life too was dominated by the richly endowed Benedictine monastery'. Chester has had its sheriffs since 1238 and by the Great Charter in the reign of Henry VII the city was constituted a county by itself and the governing body incorporated. It is now a county borough with its Mayor, Sheriff and City Council. The administrative affairs of Cheshire are in the hands of the County Council.

There have been Bishops of Chester since 1541 and among them notable men and scholars of repute. Apart from the Church of England and its ancient parishes there is an influential Roman Catholic community while the Free Churches make a distinct contribution to the religious life.

The city can offer educational advantages and there are excellent schools. The King's School was founded in 1541. Cultural interests are well catered for. A visit to the Grosvenor Museum can be amply rewarding; in the various rooms there are interesting exhibits, e.g. Roman stones and other relics; a place for an hour.

As these pages are turned over, more will be described. On the soil of Chester 'a centre of civilisation was formed which has remained through prosperity and devastation for over seventeen hundred years; occupied by different races, dominated through the centuries by differing ideals each one of which has left its impression upon the formation and the traditions of the city'. So wrote the late F. H. Crossley in his book on Cheshire. But in our day the city is not living on the past – it is moving with the times. We proceed now to look around.

We must continue with the St Werburgh misericord; it would be good if the tale could be told in the words of Henry Bradshaw, a fifteenth-century monk of the abbey, in his life of the saint, but it must be curtailed. 'When the holy vyrgyn dwelled at Wedon . . . a great multytude of wylde gees made a great destruction upon her landes. . . . The people coulde fynde no suffyeyent remedy and shewed theyr complaynte to Werburghe theyr lady.' A servant is sent to bring the wild geese but takes one for a meal! The birds come back 'mournynge and waylynge'.

> But as Wyllyam of Malmysbury sheweth
>   expresse
> The goos that was taken and stollen afore
>   away
> Was rosted and eten the same nyght doubt-
>   lesse
> So whan it was asked for upon the other day
> The bare bones were brough after this lady
>   veray
> And there by the vertue of her benedyccyon
> The byrde was restaured and flew away full
>   soone.

We see the bones on a dish, the bird flying away, while the servant confesses his guilt. Other misericords are of singular interest; careful study reveals a variety of subjects.

EXTREME LEFT There are many other carvings in these misericords, and curious figures to see. First, two grotesques at the ends of seats – a man drinking from a mug (of ale?) while an imp tries to tip it towards him. This is not an old carving but there may be a personal reminiscence which lies behind as was sometimes the case even in church carvings. Then the Elephant and Castle; this is ancient work.

LEFT Now look at the carving at the **Dean's Stall**. It is fourteenth-century work representing the Tree of Jesse and ending with the coronation of the Blessed Virgin Mary. The Jesse tree has always been a familiar subject in Christian Art, and there are many famous windows illustrative of it. In front of this carving is a pilgrim quaintly dressed. This is a magnificent bench end.

ABOVE The **High Altar** where work of enrichment was undertaken by the Friends of the Cathedral in 1957. Every generation must do what it can to enrich the House of God. The reredos is a mosaic by Antonio Salviati of *The Last Supper* and the whole ensemble is impressive. This is the focal-point of Cathedral life; the praises of God rise daily in this place with music rendered in the tradition of English cathedrals.

LEFT At the west end of the Lady Chapel – seen on the right – is the **Shrine of St Werburgh**, and this is unique to Chester. There were many shrines in the medieval churches, e.g. St Thomas à Becket at Canterbury, St Chad at Lichfield. Pilgrimage to a shrine was a pious religious act, and pilgrims came to Chester to venerate St Werburgh and kneel at the shrine, making offerings to the Abbey. The shrine has been much restored but once it provided a canopy for the feretory containing the relics. Werburgh was the daughter of King Wulfhere of Mercia in the seventh century and his wife Ermingilda and was renowned for her piety. She was buried at Hanbury in Staffordshire, but in the mid-tenth century her relics were brought to Chester. Popular religion brought pilgrims, as well, to the Holy Rood in St John's Church. Later in this book there is a view of this church which was originally a massive Norman structure.

LOWER LEFT There are many chapels in the Cathedral and regularly in use; that in the south choir aisle is dedicated to St Erasmus, an early martyr who was a popular saint in the later Middle Ages and the patron of seamen. Sometimes known as St Ermo. In this chapel lies the body of Ralph Higden the Chronicler.

RIGHT We should return to the picture in colour of **The Lady Chapel** at the east end of the Cathedral. It has recently been beautifully restored and obviously has a beauty of its own. It is early English in construction and probably dates from the time when Simon de Whitchurch was abbot (1265–91), 'the greatest and most energetic of all the abbots of Chester'. This chapel then had fewer windows and the east one had only narrow lancets. Later when the choir aisles were extended, entrances were cut into this chapel. Sad to relate, there was a time in the sixteenth century when it was used as a Consistory Court and George Marsh was tried for heresy and sent to the stake. Later the court was removed. In the nineteenth century the south choir aisle was restored, and shortened, so the entrance to the chapel on that side was closed. Further restoration went on, and in 1859 and 1872 new windows were provided. Surviving all this there is the thirteenth-century vaulting and the three remarkable bosses richly coloured. One of these is of the Holy Trinity with our Lord on the Cross, flanked by censing angels. The second is of the Blessed Virgin and Holy Child, while the third is of the martyrdom of Thomas à Becket, whose memory was venerated.

Near by is the chapel of St Werburgh in the north choir aisle, with Victorian glass above the altar. Visitors appreciate the various chapels in the Cathedral, all having distinguishing features, and their own dedications as in the south transept.

ABOVE LEFT The **North Transept**: note the Norman arch and the arcading, eleventh century. Adjacent is the tomb of John Pearson (Bishop of Chester 1673–86), a leading theologian in his time.

ABOVE RIGHT The **Chapter House** (thirteenth century). Much used by the monks to assemble and in constant use now for cathedral business, and accommodates the bookstall for the sale of guide-books, etc. Under the floor are buried the early Earls of Chester.

BELOW The unique Early English **Reader's Pulpit** in the Refectory, a capacious hall (thirteenth century).

RIGHT The **Cloister Garth,** picturesque with its pool and water-lilies. A place to relax.

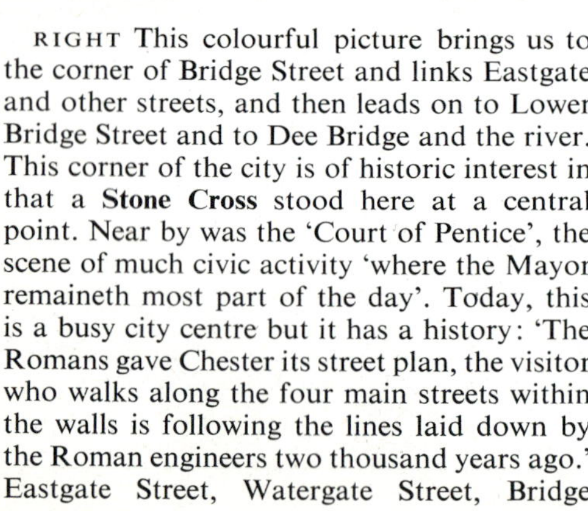

RIGHT This colourful picture brings us to the corner of Bridge Street and links Eastgate and other streets, and then leads on to Lower Bridge Street and to Dee Bridge and the river. This corner of the city is of historic interest in that a **Stone Cross** stood here at a central point. Near by was the 'Court of Pentice', the scene of much civic activity 'where the Mayor remaineth most part of the day'. Today, this is a busy city centre but it has a history: 'The Romans gave Chester its street plan, the visitor who walks along the four main streets within the walls is following the lines laid down by the Roman engineers two thousand years ago.' Eastgate Street, Watergate Street, Bridge Street and Northgate Street all converge at the Cross. But the picture has an added interest in that it shows one of the entrances to the **Rows** about which more will be said later.

At the Cross and on the opposite side of the road stands St Peter's Church, occupying the south side of the site of the Roman Pretorium. Its foundation was as far back as 907, and Domesday Book records it as a church dedicated to SS. Peter and Paul. A fifteenth-century historian wrote quaintly of this:

a paresshe church was edified truele
in honour of the aforesaid apostles twayne
which shall for ever by grace divine remayne

UPPER LEFT **Eastgate** is perhaps the busiest of all the streets with much valuable property. Beyond it is Foregate, leading out of the city; here we look towards the bridge which spans the thoroughfare and its clock. Chester is a great shopping centre, and is rapidly becoming more so, for a vast new shopping precinct has been constructed and there are the supermarkets. Redevelopment is taking place and old landmarks give place to the new. Chester is alive to modern needs and modern business. There is a spacious new Market Hall, often thronged with people keen to buy local produce – not least the delicious Cheshire cheese which has been famous for centuries.

LOWER LEFT From Eastgate one can easily walk to the Cathedral by way of **St Werburgh Street.** Then there comes into view the South Transept and Central Tower.

Passing along the south side of the Cathedral, the **Town Hall** can be seen on the west side of Northgate Street. This is very much a civic centre. Built in 1869 of red sandstone it is Gothic in style and has a tower 160 feet high – a landmark when approaching Chester. Inside the building are spacious rooms for the City of Chester District Council and its committees, and of course the Mayor's Parlour. When on view there is a fine collection of silver, as well as portraits.

ABOVE In a previous picture, and to enlighten the visitor, reference was made to the **Rows**, and one of the entrances was pointed out. Ascending by steps from the pavement, one of the Rows is reached, and if you are exploring the situation you could turn right or left and see shops in both directions. In this illustration you see what this means in actual fact, for it is a Row in Bridge Street. Long ago in the art of building Chester developed its most distinctive architectural feature in these **Rows**. It is said 'these are unique and justly world famous . . . they consist of a double tier of shops, one at ground level and the other at first floor level, each provided with a footway, the upper one being set back and covered by the second storeys of the buildings'. Quite often there are narrow passages linking the Rows and a quaintness that should not be missed. On the other hand, there are fine shops reached from them. If their origin has never been convincingly explained here is at any rate a good opportunity for shopping, and in wet weather an excellent promenade. There are antique shops with articles matching the position.

UPPER RIGHT Thinking of ancient places here (and there are many), we have already learnt something of the age of the Cathedral; the other two pictures on these pages bring us back to this.

From the city wall visitors can see the east end of the Cathedral to advantage and the Garden of Remembrance attractively laid out as the Cheshire Regiment War Memorial. The garden gives you the opportunity to relax. Within the Cathedral, in the South Transept, there is the Regimental Chapel of St George and the colours of the regiment. Here there is the Roll of Honour containing the names of 8417 men who fell in World War I and another of 715 who gave their lives in World War II.

RIGHT We now view the Cathedral's west front. When the west doors are opened a full view of the interior of the building is obtained and spectacular scenes can be witnessed: the Mayoral procession; when the Judges of the Wales and Chester Circuit attend divine service; the Bishop of Chester with the clergy; or happy brides on their way to the altar.

Adjacent was the King's School founded by Henry VIII, now rebuilt elsewhere. The Cathedral Library is housed here.

LEFT The **City Walls** are a remarkable feature of Chester. It is said this 'is the only city in England that still possesses its walls perfect in their entire circuit of two miles and so remains a splendid example of a fortified medieval town'. The first defences were made by the Roman Legion, but soon a stone wall was built, then strengthened at a later date. In the Middle Ages the walls included several towers and their appearance must have been imposing. There were the ancient gateways with their towers, and others here and there along the ramparts, put to various uses in the changing fortunes of the years. The picture (TOP LEFT) is of the tower formerly known as Newton's, standing at the north-east angle of the walls; it was also called Phoenix Tower. Rebuilt in the seventeenth century, it became known as **King Charles' Tower** because from here Charles I in 1645 watched the defeat of his forces by the Parliamentary army at Rowton Moor. This battle sealed the fate of Chester which had been Royalist and besieged. A contemporary MS. speaks of the 'sad disaster of this day'. 'The King beholds from the Phoenix Tower, from whence he removed to St Werburgh's steeple, where as he was walking with a captaine, a bullet from St John's gave him a salute, narrowly missing the King, hit the said captaine in the head, who died in the place'. This forced the king next day to leave.

The picture below it is of **The Water Tower** at the north-western angle of the walls. It stands on lower ground and formerly was surrounded by the Dee. It was built in the fourteenth century and helped to guard the port of Chester.

RIGHT The city has a deserved reputation for ancient houses that have been preserved. Here is the illustration of **God's Providence House** on the south side of Watergate Street. It was reconstructed in 1862, replacing the house in the time of the Commonwealth in the seventeenth century, but it still retains the frontal beam with the Puritan inscription. What does it mean? After the siege of Chester in the reign of Charles I – the city was predominantly Royalist but eventually fell to Cromwell's army – within a short time plague broke out and people died in great numbers. 'Grass grew both in the streets and at the high Cross'. But many were spared and it is said that in this street one house escaped the devastation; the owner inscribed his gratitude to God, and the wording still stands.

These ancient properties can all be seen and enjoyed; people with antiquarian interests will not be in a hurry to pass on. But modern interests are much with us. We look for modern buildings as well, for shops that are up-to-date catering for the needs of the moment. Alongside the old there is the new, and good hotels, splendid shops with an inviting display of goods.

GODS·PROVIDENCE·IS·MINE·INHERITANCE

ABOVE There is much historic property in Watergate Street, which at one time led to the old harbour. Antiquity confronts you on all sides. Here is **Stanley Palace**, the headquarters of the Chester branch of the English Speaking Union. It is an ancient house, rebuilt and added to, yet the old appearance remains. It was built by Peter Warburton in 1591 and later became the town house of the Stanleys of Alderney. In 1700 it was enlarged, and then remained in its old form until forty years ago, when it was completely restored. Although another wing was added, the effect is pleasing and the work was done well. Other interesting buildings include God's Providence House (already referred to) and the fascinating property on the left known as Bishop Lloyd's House. (Bishop Lloyd was Bishop of Chester from 1605 to 1615.) This is regarded as being the richest example of carved timberwork in the city. Although it has been restored, it retains an impressive appearance of age. Its panelled front bears scenes from religious history, and animals. Inside, there is some splendid panelling.

Now walk up Watergate Street towards the Cross. On your left, when you reach the Cross, is St Peter's Church. If you now turn right, you will be in Bridge Street. Like Eastgate, this is one of the principal streets for shopping and business. The Rows are along both sides, with steps up to them from ground level. There are modern shops, together with older property which has been preserved and adapted where possible. In Bridge Street is a good example of Chester's famous black-and-white timbered buildings. Its lofty, jutting façade is supported by pillars; nearby, another has the inscription 'My God, My King: My Country'. Bridge Street used to be one of the principal thoroughfares of Chester, particularly busy at holiday times and in Race Week. Chester is not alone in having had to face formidable problems with the control of traffic, but an inner ring road has now been constructed to take the bulk of the through-traffic out of the city centre. Bridge Street, though still fairly busy, especially at its lower end, is now no longer choked with motor vehicles and it is a pleasure to walk along it.

By going south, and then turning right into Grosvenor Street, you are on the way to North Wales. You pass the Grosvenor Museum and the Castle, and then cross over Grosvenor Bridge. On the way you will see the new headquarters of the County Police, housed in a fine modern building by the ring road and close to the Racecourse. Further on are the gates to Eaton Park, the estate of the Duke of Westminster.

BELOW Chester is alive to the necessity for redevelopment; you will see what this means. Yet the ancient is alongside the modern. The pleasing picture above is of the old **King's Head Inn** in Lower Bridge Street, built in 1621 by Randle Holme, 'one of the famous Chester family of antiquaries and heralds'. It has a seventeenth-century dining-room and much old timberwork inside. Near to it is Gamul House where Charles I stayed during the siege of Chester.

At this point a walk up Castle Street will lead to the ancient church, now disused, of **St Mary's** on the Hill, near to the Castle. Built in red sandstone it has an imposing tower. Its interior is impressive, the nave, chancel, aisles and panelled roof; then two altar tombs, one of Thomas Gamul, Recorder of Chester in 1613, and his wife.

In the north aisle there is a monument to the memory of the Randle Holme family. Then, beyond, is the **Castle of Chester** built originally in the eleventh century and having a fine forcourt and entrance. There has been much rebuilding and now the County Hall adjoins. The Crown Court sits in the Castle.

ABOVE Chester abounds in interesting properties. Quite apart from the Roman remains which can be seen in the neighbourhood of the Newgate, there are old houses to look at and the best of these have been preserved, exteriors redecorated and generally kept in good repair. There are properties in black-and-white with the woodwork treated accordingly. Several of these are now hostels or inns where once they were town houses of the well-to-do. Evidence of this is in the region of Bridge Street, Lower Bridge Street, and leading to the riverside.

The Falcon Café is in Lower Bridge Street. Parts are old (1626) and there is an earlier stone basement. Observe the long window on the first floor, a feature of local architecture, as is the case with other buildings hereabout. All around there are these properties with quaint alleys and names which indicate they were linked with various trades and trade guilds, e.g. Mercers' Row, Shoemakers' Row.

RIGHT A very good example of property reaching back to antiquity is the **Bear and Billet Inn** with its façade dated 1664. This was once the town house of the Earls of Shrewsbury, Serjeants of the Bridgegate. This is on the west side; on the east side of the street there is Tudor House – also of the seventeenth century and containing interesting features – open to the public.

WORTHINGTON'S
ALES
ONLY
ON DRAUGHT

ABOVE **Bridgegate.** Five gates linked up the city walls, and Bridgegate guarded the Dee Bridge. Passing through it one can walk along, see the boating and go up the river. 'Without the consanguinity of Chester and Dee both would lose in significance and attractiveness.' The Mayor is still Admiral of the Dee.

BELOW **The Old Dee Bridge.** Originally built in the thirteenth century, a bridge with a history and rather fine. There are good views at this point: the Regatta, Head of the River Race bring the crowds – but fishing must not be forgotten.

RIGHT **St John's Church.** It is rewarding to visit it and see the fine Norman pillars and the masonry generally. The ruins of a much larger building are well preserved. Over the centuries it has had a renowned history and for a time in the eleventh century was the Cathedral Church.

ABOVE Before we finish we look at this illustration of black-and-white half-timbered houses. It is in Park Street, not ancient but close to almshouses which are old, though reconditioned. To see these one must walk a short distance to the Newgate; Park Street adjoins. There is an advantage in this, for on the east side of the gate on both sides of the road there are Roman remains laid out effectively in gardens; part of the old High Cross and Roman columns. Just beyond, work is proceeding to excavate and restore a part of the Roman Amphitheatre. Further on beyond St John's Church there is the beautiful Grosvenor Park.

There is more in Chester that can make the stay here an enjoyable time. The Zoological Gardens at Upton are quite accessible: a splendid Zoo in an attractive setting.

We have looked at the Cathedral. In things ecclesiastical, placenames recall the existence of religious houses in medieval days, etc.: Black Friars, Grey Friars, White Friars and Nuns' Road all indicative of Orders of Friars, and St Mary's Priory a convent of nuns.

We have looked at Chester but not at everything – only a selection. What was said of another historic place is equally applicable to this city: 'Linger awhile amid its historic charm'.